Breath Prayers for Anxiety

Esther Gillie

ISBN:9798637891955

DEDICATION

To all of us who experience anxiety in the normal course of living.
May God grant us peace as only God can give.

CONTENTS

INTRODUCTION

Everyone feels anxious now and then, particularly during trying times such as economic challenges, illness, pandemics, disasters, trauma and other life events. Breath prayers are an effective way to keep your perspective and help you remain calm in the face of change and unexpected stress. These simple prayers are anchored in Scriptures that help remind us of God's presence and give us hope in the midst of chaos.

This book offers three sections: God's Character, What God Provides, and What God Says About Me. Each area of focus offers encouraging and uplifting prayers based on Bible verses that help put things in perspective. These prayers remind us of how great God is, what God is like, how God cares for us, and who we are as children of God. Words of hope offer a refreshing alternative to the negative and overwhelming messages so often encountered in a challenging situation.

ANXIETY

Anxiety: that feeling that we are in danger, that we are facing a threat, some event or experience with an uncertain outcome, something over which we feel we have no control. Everyone experiences anxiety to some extent, whether it is worry, uneasiness, nervousness, or outright fear. It is a normal part of life, especially during times of stress, serious illness, economic impact, pandemics, disasters and other life events. Sometimes, people experience panic attacks or develop an anxiety disorder that interferes with their ability to function, and they need to seek professional help.

Whenever you feel anxious, for whatever reason, one highly effective method of coping is prayer, connecting with the God who created us, loves us, understands us, helps us, and is always with us. Scripture is filled with God's promises to us, reminding us of who God is, who we are, and how God cares for us. This book offers some simple breath prayers based on Scripture verses that can help calm us when we feel anxious, and help us focus on God's promises.

WHAT ARE BREATH PRAYERS?

Breath prayers are short prayers, usually based on Scriptures, which help people be aware of God's presence. They are short phrases of petition that are linked to the breathing process. Breath prayers were known to the early church fathers and mothers as a way to pray without ceasing. These easy-to-recall two-part phrases are prayed in rhythm with a person's breathing, and remind the person praying of who God is and how much God cares for them. Breath prayers can be prayed anywhere – in a car, a classroom, at home, in a grocery store, a doctor's office, a friend's place – anywhere feelings of anxiety might arise.

How do breath prayers work?

These simple, easy-to-remember prayers help people regain perspective, and reconnect with the promises of God, bringing calm, peace, encouragement, strength and hope in times of distress.

How to pray a breath prayer

Get as comfortable and relaxed as possible. Close your eyes if you can. Focus on your breathing. Breathe in as deeply as you can. Exhale slowly. Continue breathing with intention and focus. When you are ready to pray, think/pray the first part of the prayer as you inhale. Think/pray the second part of the prayer as you exhale. In the written prayer, a forward slash (/) will mark suggested places in the wording of the prayer for the inhale (before the forward slash) and exhale (after the forward slash).

Once people are comfortable with this method of praying, they can create their own meaningful breath prayers which address the particular situation they are facing or relate to a meaningful passage of Scripture.

God bless you as you pray!

GOD'S CHARACTER

God / loves me

(John 3:16)

~~~~~~~~~~~~~~~~~

God / cares for me

(1 Peter 5:7)

~~~~~~~~~~~~~~~~~

God / strengthens me

(Exodus 15:2)

God / is with me

(Psalm 23:4)

+++++++++++++

God / is good

(Mark 10:18)

+++++++++++++

God / remembers me

(Isaiah 49:15)

God / is for me

(Romans 8:31)

···

God / hears me

(1 John 5:14)

···

God / answers me

(Psalm 34:4)

God / delivers me

(Psalm 50:15)

God / helps me

(Isaiah 41:10)

<<<<<<<<<<<<<<<

God / provides for me

(Psalm 23:1)

God / calls me by name

(Isaiah 43:1)

> > > > > > > > > > > > > >

God / rescues me

(Isaiah 35:4)

> > > > > > > > > > > > > >

God / lifts me up

(1 Peter 5:6)

God / comforts me

(Isaiah 49:13)

##############

God is / near

(Philippians 4:5)

##############

God / created everything

(Genesis 1)

God / created me

(Psalm 139:13)

God / is eternal

(Psalm 90:2)

God / is just

(Job 34:12)

God's kingdom / cannot be shaken

(Hebrews 12:28)

WHAT GOD PROVIDES

God's Word / does not fail

(Luke 1:37)

===================

God gives me / peace

(John 14:27)

===================

God gives me / joy

(Psalm 94:10)

God gives me / rest

(Matthew 11:28)

`````````````````````````````````

# God gives me / hope

(Psalm 62:5)

`````````````````````````````````

God gives me / a future

(Jeremiah 29:11)

God gives me / a sound mind

(2 Timothy 1:7)

OOOOOOOOOOOOOOO

God knows / what I need

(Matthew 6:32)

OOOOOOOOOOOOOO

God gives me / what I need

(Philippians 4:19)

God does / what I cannot do

(2 Corinthians 12:10)

ccccccccccccc

God has / a plan for me

(Psalm 139:16)

ccccccccccccc

God renews / my strength

(Isaiah 40:31)

God rejoices / over me

(Zephaniah 3:17)

****

God is / on my side

(Psalm 118:6)

****

God / makes a way of escape

(1 Corinthians 10:13)

With God / all things are possible

(Matthew 19:26)

<<<<<<<<<<<<<<<<

God / never leaves me

(Genesis 28:15)

<<<<<<<<<<<<<<<<

God / forgives me

(Matthew 9:6)

God / heals me

(Psalm 30:2)

>>>>>>>>>>>>>>>>

God / knows me

(Psalm 139)

>>>>>>>>>>>>>>>>>

God / is in control

(Philippians 3:20-21)

God is / my friend

(John 15:14)

God is / my Father

(Romans 4:16)

God / watches over me

(Psalm 121:3)

God / protects me

(Psalm 121:7)

WHAT GOD SAYS ABOUT ME

I can do / all things through Christ

(Philippians 4:13)

++++++++++++++

I trust / in God

(Proverbs 3:5)

++++++++++++++

Nothing / can separate me from God

(Romans 8:39)

When I am afraid / I trust in God

(Psalm 56:3)

~~~~~~~~~~~~~~

God has not given me / a spirit of fear

(Psalm 27:1)

~~~~~~~~~~~~~~

When I am anxious / God consoles me

(Psalm 64:19)

I am valuable / to God

(Matthew 10:31)

....

I am / more than a conqueror

(Romans 8:37)

....

I have / the mind of Christ

(I Corinthians 2:16)

I am / God's child

(Acts 17:28)

=================

I am / healed

(Exodus 15:26)

=================

My whole being / hopes in God

(Psalm 130:5)

I am / thankful to God

(I Chronicles 29:13)

////////////////////////////////

My help / comes from God

(Psalm 121:2)

INDEX OF BIBLE VERSES

Old Testament	Psalms	New Testament
Genesis 1	Psalm 27:1	Matthew 6:32
Genesis 28:15	Psalm 23:1	Matthew 9:6
Exodus 15:2	Psalm 23:4	Matthew 10:31
Exodus 15:26	Psalm 30:2	Matthew 11:28
I Chronicles 29:13	Psalm 34:4	Matthew 19:26
Job 34:12	Psalm 46:1	Mark 10:18
Proverbs 3:5	Psalm 50:15	Luke 1:37
Isaiah 35:4	Psalm 56:3	John 3:16
Isaiah 40:31	Psalm 63:5	John 14:27
Isaiah 41:10	Psalm 64:19	John 15:14
Isaiah 41:13	Psalm 90:2	Acts 17:28
Isaiah 43:1	Psalm 91:14	Romans 4:16
Isaiah 49:13	Psalm 94:10	Romans 8:31
Isaiah 49:15	Psalm 118:6	Romans 8:37
Jeremiah 29:11	Psalm 121:2	Romans 8:39
Zephaniah 3:17	Psalm 121:3	1 Corinthians 10:13

Old Testament	Psalms	New Testament
	Psalm 121:7	1 Corinthians 2:16
	Psalm 130:5	2 Corinthians 12:10
	Psalm 139	Philippians 3:20-21
	Psalm 139:13	Philippians 4:5
	Psalm 139:16	Philippians 4:13
		Philippians 4:19
		2 Timothy 1:7
		Hebrews 12:28
		1 Peter 5:6
		1 Peter 5:7
		1 John 5:14

ABOUT THE AUTHOR

Dr. Gillie is the current Dean of Regent University Library. She also serves as an adjunct professor for the School of Divinity at Regent University and facilitates coursework in spiritual formation. Dr. Gillie attended Northeastern Seminary where she completed her M.Div. and D.Min. degrees.